AUTISM
IN MY FAMILY

of related interest

Tomas Loves
A rhyming book about fun,
friendship – and autism
Jude Welton
Illustrated by Jane Telford
ISBN 978 1 84905 544 4
eISBN 978 0 85700 969 2

Can I tell you about Autism?
A guide for friends, family and professionals
Jude Welton
Illustrated by Jane Telford
ISBN 978 1 84905 453 9
eISBN 978 0 85700 829 9

Babies Are Noisy
A book for big brothers and sisters
including those on the autism spectrum
Anne-Marie Harrison
Illustrated by Beth Byrne
ISBN 978 1 84905 459 1
eISBN 978 0 85700 835 0

Brotherly Feelings
Me, My Emotions, and My Brother
with Asperger's Syndrome
Sam Frender and Robin Schiffmiller
ISBN 978 1 84310 850 4
eISBN 978 1 84642 594 3

AUTISM
IN MY FAMILY

A JOURNAL FOR SIBLINGS
OF CHILDREN WITH ASD

Sandra Tucker

Foreword by Catherine Faherty

Jessica Kingsley *Publishers*
London and Philadelphia

Material kindly reproduced from *Autism… What Does It Mean To Me?* by Catherine Faherty (Future Horizons, 2014)

First published in 2017
by Jessica Kingsley Publishers
73 Collier Street
London N1 9BE, UK
and
400 Market Street, Suite 400
Philadelphia, PA 19106, USA

www.jkp.com

Library of Congress Cataloging in Publication Data
Title: Autism in my family : a journal for siblings of children with ASD / Sandra Tucker.
Description: London ; Philadelphia : Jessica Kingsley Publishers, 2017. | Audience: Age 8-12. | Audience: Grade 4 to 6.
Identifiers: LCCN 2017002423 (print) | LCCN 2017005114 (ebook) | ISBN 9781785927072 (alk. paper) | ISBN 9781784502645 (ebook)
Subjects: LCSH: Autism in children--Juvenile literature. | Autistic children--Education--Juvenile literature.
Classification: LCC RJ506.A9 T83 2017 (print) | LCC RJ506.A9 (ebook) | DDC 618.92/85882--dc23

British Library Cataloguing in Publication Data
A CIP catalogue record for this book is available from the British Library

ISBN 978 1 78592 707 2
eISBN 978 1 78450 264 5

Printed and bound in the United States

CONTENTS

Foreword

I am pleased to introduce *Autism In My Family* to siblings of children with autism, their families, therapists, and the autism community at large. Back in the fall of 2014 I received an email message from Sandra Tucker telling me about her idea to create a book for families to accompany my books, *Aspergers...What Does It Mean To Me?* (Future Horizons, 2000) and it's update, *Autism...What Does It Mean To Me?* (Future Horizons, 2014). My books feature workbook pages promoting self-understanding for the autistic child and teen. Sandra explained that this new book would be patterned after my books for children with ASD, but it would be focused on their brothers and sisters. Initially, I was impressed with the fact that she wrote to me (we did not know each other); and was intrigued with her proposal. After hearing more about her ideas and experience, I was positively thrilled.

I learned that Sandra founded and directs the organization, Sibling Tree, engaging siblings of all ages in understanding themselves related to their unique perspective and position in their families. Sandra herself, grew up with two brothers – one of whom is on the autism spectrum. Her passion is to empower boys and girls, helping them communicate within their family structure about their own experiences, thoughts, feelings, and ideas; to allow their natural resilience to blossom; and to give them the confidence and the tools to become effective advocates for their siblings on the autism spectrum. Along the way, these children discover that they are not alone – that in fact they are a part of a growing movement of siblings across the country and across the world.

Following the same twelve chapters found in my books, the topics range from School, Understanding, People, Feeling Upset, Happiness, and more. Keeping my workbook idea, the young readers of this new book are encouraged to independently fill in some pages, while other pages are meant for the child and parent to explore together. In addition, I was delighted to hear her proposal for a brand new feature. Siblings are invited to join, share, and learn along with other siblings across the country and the world, via her website, www.sandraellentucker.com. This optional opportunity is a wonderful support for girls and boys interested in expanding their world in a safe way – a world in which they may too often feel alone.

Sandra's compassion and empathy for typical and autistic siblings and their families is impressive and humbling. I am thrilled that Sandra has created such empathetic support in this book for her fellow siblings. If you are a parent, you have in your hands a wonderful guide to help you support your typical daughters and sons as they grow. Therapists will appreciate this tool to add to therapy sessions. And I imagine that as siblings grow and mature, they will come to accept, embrace, and treasure the personal exploration available to them through this wonderful book.

I invite you look through these pages to experience Sandra Tucker's passion, focus, and commitment to this unique and potentially group – your typically-developing children. They may become powerful agents-of-change for the larger society's acceptance and celebration of diversity.

Catherine Faherty
Autism Specialist, Mentor, Teacher Trainer
TEACCH® Certified Advanced Consultant
Authorized Carol Gray Social Stories™ Instructor
Author of the books: *Autism…What Does
It Mean To Me?* Future Horizons, 2014
Understanding Death and Illness and What They Teach About Life, Future
Horizons 2009, (Autism Society of America 2009 Book of the Year)
Communication: What Does It Mean To Me? Future Horizons, 2010

How to Use this Book

What do the symbols ♥, ▲ and ● mean in this book?

On the top left hand corner of some pages, you will see these symbols.

When you see ♥, it means that the authors of this book want you to invite a parent to work with you on that page.

When you see ▲, it means that the authors of this book want you to invite your entire family to work with you on that page.

When you see ●, it means that the authors of this book want you to invite your brother/sister to work with you on that page.

How do I use this book?

This book is for you to learn more about yourself, as a sibling of a brother or sister with autism.

Feel free to draw, write, paste, cut or use any other creative way you would like to express yourself. When it says to WRITE IT. DRAW IT. PASTE IT. you can write your feelings/answer, draw how you feel or a representation of the answer, or paste images that represent how you feel or the answer.

If you want to share your pages with other siblings in the world, you can upload pictures of your pages to www.sandraellentucker.com. This page will also share answers that other siblings have had and share resources that are just for you!

Chapter One

INTRODUCTION

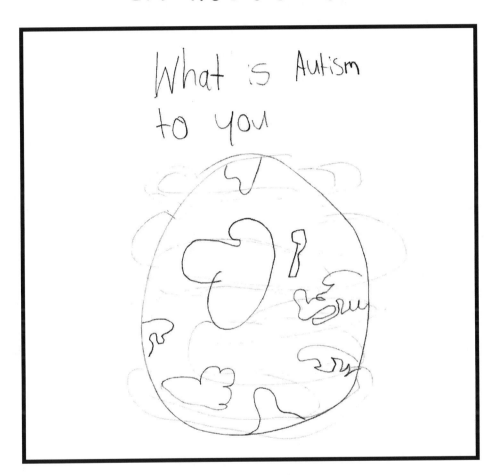

What is Autism to you

WORKBOOK

I AM...

My name is . . . .

My birthday is . . . .

My favorite thing about myself is . . . .

. . . .

. . . .

Below I will paste or draw a picture of myself:

Date . . . .

MY SIBLINGS ARE...

My siblings' names are. . . . .

. . . .

Their birthdays are . . . .

. . . .

My favorite thing about each of them is. . . . .

. . . .

. . . .

. . . .

Below I will paste or draw a picture of my siblings:

WHAT IS AUTISM TO YOU?!

WRITE IT. DRAW IT. PASTE IT.

Date . . . .

THE BEGINNING

When my brother/sister was . . . . . . years old, my parents did
not understand why he/she . . . .

. . . .

. . . .

How old was my brother/sister when he/she was diagnosed?

. . . .

How did you explain autism to him/her?

. . . .

. . . .

How did you explain autism to me?

. . . .

. . . .

How did you feel through this?

. . . .

. . . .

. . . .

THE BEGINNING (CONTINUED)

I started to notice that my brother/sister was different when he/she . . . .

. . . .

. . . .

I remember my parents describing autism to me by saying

. . . .

. . . .

. . . .

I felt . . . .

. . . .

. . . .

Here are questions that we still have about autism: . . . .

. . . .

. . . .

. . . .

. . . .

IDENTITY FIRST VS PERSON FIRST

Identity First:

- Being autistic is important to who they are.

- It is how they think and communicate and how they understand the world and other people.

- Autism cannot be separated from who they are.

Person First:

- Autism is a part of who they are, but that is not necessarily an important part of who they are.

- It is something separate from themselves.

Talk to your family about the different wording.

How does it make everyone feel for each word and why?

. . . .

. . . .

. . . .

What does the family prefer to use?

. . . .

. . . .

Chapter Two

THE SENSORY EXPERIENCE

WORKBOOK

The Five Senses

Write down what you hear right now.

Describe your favourite smell.

Draw the tastiest food.

Glue something to the page that has a texture you enjoy.

Glue something to the page that you like to see.

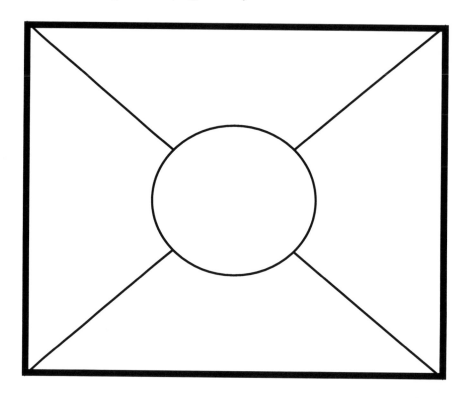

Date . . . .

LOUD OR SUDDEN NOISES

I will circle the sounds that are too loud for me:

Car Horns   *People Yelling*   *Dogs Barking*   *Music*

Sirens   *Someone Typing*   *Television*   *Siblings*

Other . . . .

When I hear these sounds, they make me feel . . . .

. . . .

. . . .

I have noticed my brother/sister doesn't like these sounds . . . .

. . . .

. . . .

. . . .

When they hear these sounds, they react by. . . . .

. . . .

. . . .

. . . .

'QUIET' SOUNDS OTHERS DON'T NOTICE

There are some sounds that some people with autism notice that other people do not hear, or they do not pay attention to. People call them quiet sounds.

Examples are:

- Insects.

- Fluorescent lights, fans, refrigerators, computers.

- Airplanes or engines far away.

- Radio or TV sounds in other rooms.

- Background musical tracks in movies.

- People talking or working in other rooms.

- People breathing or turning the pages of a book.

- People chewing or scratching.

Most people may not pay attention to these kinds of sounds, because they seem quiet or unimportant to them. They might ignore these sounds. Many people with autism cannot ignore some of these sounds. Some of these sounds bother me, even though I don't have autism.

WRITE IT. DRAW IT. PASTE IT. Below I will describe what quiet sounds bother me or ones that I noticed bother my brother/sister with autism:

'Quiet' Sounds Others Don't Notice (Continued)

Roll up a regular sheet of paper. Put one end at your ear. In the other end, have your parent whisper "quiet" sounds into your ear. Then try to answer these math problems while they are doing this.

125+310=

34+23=

4X3=

Did you have a hard time concentrating? . . . .

WRITE IT. DRAW IT. PASTE IT. How did you feel during this?

TOUCHING

Below I will glue a texture that I love to touch. I will write how I feel when I touch it.

Below I will glue a texture I touch every day. I will write how I feel when I touch it.

Below I will glue a texture I don't like to feel. I will write how I feel when I touch it.

Date . . . .

TOUCHING (CONTINUED)

Just like sounds, people with autism have heightened senses towards textures. Sometimes things will make their skin feel tingly or painful.

Below I will glue a texture that my brother/sister loves to touch. I will write how they feel when they touch it.

Below I will glue a texture that my brother/sister touches every day. I will write how they feel when they touch it.

Below I will write a texture that my brother/sister doesn't like to touch. I will write how they feel when they touch it.

ODORS

WRITE IT. DRAW IT. PASTE IT. I will close my eyes and smell the scents around me.

I would describe them as . . . .

. . . .

. . . .

I will circle what is true for me and highlight what is true for my brother/sister:

- I pay attention to odors a lot.

- I usually want to smell things I see or touch.

- I like to smell people's hair or their skin.

- The odors of perfume or some deodorants bother me.

- If an odor is strong, I can't think about anything else.

WRITE IT. DRAW IT. PASTE IT. When I smell something that overwhelms me, it can make it difficult for me to concentrate or:

Date . . . .

SEEING

<u>WRITE IT. DRAW IT. PASTE IT.</u> Below are things that I can see from where I am:

Now I will close my eyes, count to ten and open them.

<u>WRITE IT. DRAW IT. PASTE IT.</u> Below are things that I see now, that I did not realize I saw before:

Many people with autism see things that other people might not notice. Some people with autism get confused or anxious when there are too many things to see at the same time.

TASTING

WRITE IT. DRAW IT. PASTE IT. Some of my favorite things to taste are:

My favorite things about these are:

- The way it tastes.

- The color of it.

- How it feels in my mouth.

Circle what you pay attention to when you eat:

- The texture – how it feels in your mouth.

- The flavor – how it tastes.

- The color.

- Trying new things.

- Tasting the same thing.

What are your brother/sister's favorite things to taste?

. . . .

What is the strangest thing that your brother/sister likes to taste?

. . . .

Physical Pain

Some people with autism are very sensitive to pain.

Circle what is true for you and highlight what is true for your brother/sister:

- I rarely notice pain. I might be injured and not notice.

- I am very sensitive to pain. It's very easy for me to feel hurt.

- When I am focused on something, I don't notice anything else.

- I like cold.

- I like heat.

- I like to feel pain.

- I usually don't feel pain.

Examples of things that cause pain are:

- Touching a hot burner on the stove.

- Touching water that is too hot or too cold.

- Dropping something heavy on your foot.

- Eating food that is too hot.

- Closing a door on your fingers.

Date . . . .

WRITE IT. DRAW IT. PASTE IT. Below are things that cause us pain:

STIMMING

Stimming is a short way of saying "self-stimulation."

People with autism sometimes stim more than people who do not have autism. It may help you to focus, relax or calm down. An example of stimming is hand flapping, shaking your leg, or playing with your hair.

When I need to focus or relax, I . . . .

. . . .

. . . .

. . . .

. . . .

I will share with my parents what I do to focus and/or relax and ask my parents what they do. We will list some new ideas below:

. . . .

. . . .

. . . .

. . . .

. . . .

EMOTIONAL PAIN

As a sibling of an individual with autism, I sometimes feel sadness, anger, frustration, embarrassment, etc.

We will share with each other five feelings we had this week and why we felt that way.

Below are some ways we can manage those feelings:

EMOTIONAL PAIN (CONTINUED)

Now work together to create a sibling toolbox. Inside the toolbox, you can put a journal where you can write down when you feel different things and why. Pick a place in your house where you can leave the journal when you want your parents to read it. Your parents can then respond to what you wrote in the journal and put it back in that safe place.

Include some of your favorite things to touch, smell, taste, listen to, or look at that will make you smile. This will be for you to use whenever you are scared, worried, angry, etc.

Include some of the different things that you came up with to manage those feelings.

Parents: Consider creating an emergency plan that can be placed in this toolbox to relieve some of the sibling's anxiety. An example of this plan is on the next page.

Sibling Toolbox Emergency Plan

If something is happening that is overwhelming for me but I am safe, I can call:

Name: **Aunt Sandra**

Phone Number: **555-123-4567**

If my brother/sister needs to go to the hospital, I will go with **Aunt Sandra** until everything is okay.

If I am afraid, I can tell my parent by doing or saying:

Write a note and put it in my parent's hand. I will then go back to my room.

They will then:

Call **Aunt Sandra** to pick me up or one of them will take me for ice cream.

Chapter Three

WAYS OF THINKING

WORKBOOK

FOCUSED INTERESTS

Everyone has interests – things they like. One of the things about autism is that it helps my brother/sister focus on their interests. When they focus on these interests, they usually feel pretty good. I can have focused interests as well.

WRITE IT. DRAW IT. PASTE IT. My brother/sister's current focused interests are:

WRITE IT. DRAW IT. PASTE IT. My current focused interests are:

FOCUSED INTERESTS (CONTINUED)

As a sibling, there are times when my brother/sister's focus on interests can cause different feelings such as pride, frustration, confusion, or hurt.

A time when I felt proud of their interests was . . . .

. . . .

A time when I felt frustration over their interests was. . . . .

. . . .

A time when I felt confusion over their interests was . . . .

. . . .

A time when I felt hurt over their interests was. . . . .

. . . .

Tell us another time when you felt a different emotion:

. . . .

. . . .

. . . .

. . . .

WAYS TO LEARN

Sometimes learning comes easily and quickly, and sometimes learning takes more time. This is true for all children, teenagers, and adults. People learn best in different ways – each in their own way.

I will circle or highlight what is true for me.

My best ways to learn are by:

- Watching other people before I try something new.

- Getting information from photos or pictures.

- Reading about it.

- Listening to people tell me about it.

- Thinking about how it fits into my focused interest.

- Talking to others about what I am learning.

- Writing about what I am learning.

- Making things related to what I am learning.

- Staying focused on it, so I do not have to do other things.

- Experimenting and figuring things out by myself.

- Asking people questions.

- Having people type the answers so I can read them, because it's better than listening to someone tell me about it.

- Listening to someone talk, because it's better for me to listen than to read what they type.

- Learning some other way. I like learning when:

. . . .

. . . .

. . . .

. . . .

PERFECTION

Sometimes as a sibling, I want to be perfect so that I don't cause any more stress for my parents. There are also times where I want to be perfect so that I can get the same attention as my brother or sister with autism. There might be times that I do something similar to my brother/sister but don't get the same reaction that they get. This isn't because I didn't do as well; some things are more difficult for my brother/sister to do than they are for me.

WRITE IT. DRAW IT. PASTE IT. I worry about being perfect when:

Everything cannot always be perfect. I am not wrong or bad if other people are first or if I make a mistake. Everyone makes mistakes – even the smartest people in the world.

When I feel like I am trying too hard to be perfect, I can:

- Talk to my parents.

- Remind myself that mistakes are okay.

- Remind myself that I am different than my brother/sister.

- Talk to other siblings about how I feel.

PERFECTION VERSUS DOING YOUR BEST

Does "doing your best" mean having to be perfect?

The answer is "no." Doing your best does not mean having to be perfect. All humans make mistakes sometimes, even when they are doing their best. No one does everything perfectly right all the time.

When someone says "Do your best," it is meant as a reminder to work carefully and to try to keep my attention on what I am doing. A person can do his or her best and still make mistakes. It is okay to make mistakes. In fact, making mistakes is a necessary part of learning!

WRITE IT. DRAW IT. PASTE IT. Below I will put something that I want to be perfect and then I will put how it would look if it wasn't perfect. I will think about the good things that come from things not going perfectly.

Routines and Familiarity

Most people like routines and familiarity. A routine is when I do the same things in the same ways. Familiarity means being used to something because of seeing or doing it previously. Familiar things are not new.

Routines can feel especially good because I know what to expect.

Do you like to know what is going to happen and when it will happen? How do you feel when things don't happen the way they're supposed to?

. . . .

. . . .

Does your brother/sister like to know what is going to happen and when it will happen? How do they react when things don't happen the way they're supposed to?

. . . .

. . . .

Sometimes things change. Unexpected things happen in life. Sometimes people know ahead of time that things will change.

Would you feel better if you knew ahead of time that there will be a change to the plan?

. . . .

Schedules

My brother/sister with autism can have multiple appointments so it is hard to know what is going on. A schedule is a list of what is going to happen. I will create a schedule each month with my parents.

A schedule will help me know:

- Days I will spend with my parents by myself.

- Days when I will have to wait during an appointment so that I bring something fun and new to do.

- Days I can spend time with friends or family.

We can create a schedule by:

- Using a typical calendar, a notebook, a clipboard, or a binder.

- List the events for the day in sequence.

- Adding pictures for certain events.

- Highlighting events that are for me.

- Putting the calendar in a place that is easy for us all to find.

This schedule can be used by the entire family or made for just me.

WRITE IT. DRAW IT. PASTE IT. Below are some things that I want to have included on the schedule:

Chapter Four

Talent and Creative Expression

WORKBOOK

MUSIC

Many people like to listen to music. Some people can express themselves more easily when they make music than when they use words.

Some children and adults have perfect pitch and a natural ability to sing or play a musical instrument. They might have very sensitive hearing.

WRITE IT. DRAW IT. PASTE IT. I use music to express myself by:

DRAMA

Drama is an art form that many people enjoy. Some people like to go see movies, plays, and musicals.

Actors must pretend that they are someone else. Actors are skilled at observing and copying how people move and how they sound.

I will create a short play about being a sibling that I can act out for my family. I can write my play below.

. . . .

. . . .

. . . .

. . . .

. . . .

. . . .

. . . .

. . . .

. . . .

. . . .

DRAWING

The act of drawing and looking at drawings adds to the beauty and enjoyment of life.

Drawing can bring out a world that people can only imagine, can recreate a memory, or give individuals an opportunity to express their emotions in a way they might not have been able to with words.

Below is a drawing that expresses an emotion that I have felt:

PAINTING

Painting pictures and spending time looking at paintings adds to the beauty and enjoyment of life.

Painting is similar to drawing. When you paint, you use many different colors, paints, textures, and canvases to create images.

Below is a painting that represents who I am:

PHOTOGRAPHY AND FILMMAKING

Photography and filmmaking are forms of art that require the use of cameras. There are many different types of cameras. Just like other art forms, there are many styles of photography and filmmaking. There are forms of art that require the artist to use his or her eyes; it is a visual form of art.

Ask your parents/guardians to help you take a picture or create a short film that represents your family. You can paste the photo below or share the film online.

WRITING

Writing includes stories, essays, poetry, e-mail messages, blog posts, and other kinds of writing. Writing can help the writers and the people who read their writing think clearly, appreciate beauty in the world, laugh, cry, dream, and imagine new things.

Writing includes using pens, pencils, and/or keyboards. Sometimes it is easier to communicate by writing, rather than talking.

Below I will share a story, write a letter, or create a poem to share a feeling:

. . . .

. . . .

. . . .

. . . .

. . . .

. . . .

. . . .

. . . .

. . . .

. . . .

COMICS

Creating comics usually combines drawing and writing. Some children and adults are good at creating comics. Some comics are funny, but they don't have to be funny. Some comics are serious. Some comics simply express the artist's ideas. Children and adults who like to draw and write comics find it to be a good way to express their ideas, experiences, concerns, and/or questions.

Create a comic below or paste a comic that you enjoy. If you're not sure where to find a comic, you can ask your parents for help in finding one in their newspaper or online.

MAKING THINGS

Making things includes building, constructing, and assembling. It includes using materials like Lego®, wood, metal, paper, plastic, cloth, clay, and other materials. It includes what is called "fabric art," such as sewing, embroidery, knitting, crocheting, and other needlework. It includes activities that are referred to as "crafts," such as using clay or other materials. It includes the use of specific tools. This talent may also be used for the drawing of designs, plans, and blueprints, before actually making something.

Many children and adults are skilled and talented at one or more of these ways of making things.

I will make something and paste it here or take a picture of what I made and paste it here.

COOKING

Some people enjoy cooking. They may be interested in cooking certain types of food. They may be interested in baking cookies, cakes, and pies. Many professional cooks regard the act of cooking to be a combination of art and science.

Paste the recipe for your favorite food here. You can also ask your parent/guardian to help you cook a favorite food. Take a picture of your favorite creation.

MECHANICAL PROJECTS

Many people have good mechanical ability. They might like to figure out how things work. They might like to take things apart. They might like to put things together.

WRITE IT. DRAW IT. PASTE IT. Below are things that I can take apart and put back together or some things that I would like to figure out how they work:

Computers, Tablets, and Other Technology

Working with technology requires specific abilities.

Computers are literal, concrete, and predictable. A computer program follows its rules, exactly. Working with technology, like tablets, computers, and other technical developments, might come naturally and easily to some people.

Share some of your favorite ways to use technology or things that you would like to learn about technology:

. . . .

. . . .

. . . .

. . . .

. . . .

. . . .

. . . .

. . . .

. . . .

Date . . . .

Many Other Ways

Being "creative" means to imagine and make things, to do things in unique ways, or to invent something different or new. There are many other ways of expressing yourself creatively. Other examples of creative expression are collage, quilting, applique, sculpture, woodworking, designing and building bicycles or vehicles, architecture, and arranging furniture in rooms of the house.

Share some other ways to express creativity:

. . . .

. . . .

. . . .

. . . .

Create a collage of images that make you feel creative.

BROTHER/SISTER WITH AUTISM

Now that you have discovered your talents, think about what talents your brother/sister with autism has. Circle the talents below that might be their talent and cross out the ones they wouldn't like. Write or change why it could be their talent or write why they might not like it.

Music because they might have sensitive hearing.

. . . .

Drama because they are skilled at observing and copying other people.

. . . .

Drawing and painting because they are visual thinkers and automatically see pictures in their mind.

. . . .

Photography and filmmaking because they see things in interesting ways and have excellent visual skills.

. . . .

Writing because they communicate more naturally and easily by writing on paper or with a keyboard, rather than talking.

. . . .

Creating **comics** because they enjoy drawing and writing to express their ideas, experiences, concerns, and/or questions.

. . . .

Making things because they enjoy building, constructing, and/or assembling things.

. . . .

Cooking because they enjoy combining art and science.

. . . .

Mechanical projects because they like to take things apart or put things together.

. . . .

Computers, tablets, and other technology because they like things that are literal, concrete, and predictable.

. . . .

Many other ways

. . . .

. . . .

. . . .

. . . .

Chapter Five

PEOPLE

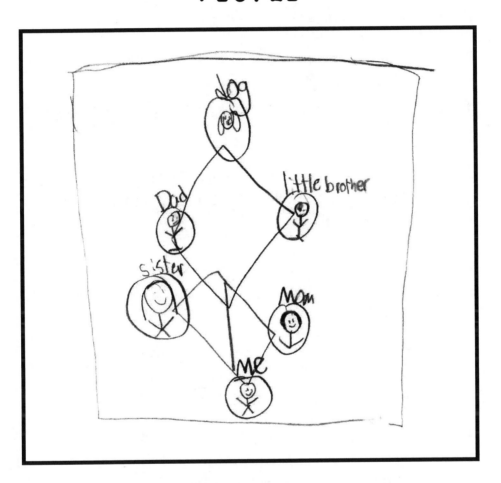

WORKBOOK

ROLES

Everyone has a role. At school, my role is to be a student. When I am with my mom and dad, I am their son or daughter. When I am at a friend's house, I am their friend/guest.

People can have more than one role at a time. When I am at home, I can be a son/daughter, brother/sister, student while doing my homework, and teacher if I am helping my sibling with a new task.

Below are a few roles that people might take on. I will circle the role that describes me. I will highlight the roles that describe someone else in my family.

Son/Daughter	Shopper
Brother/Sister	Comedian
Student	Hug Giver
Cook	TV Watcher
Dish Washer	Music Player
Babysitter	Bike Rider
Helper	Brother/Sister Translator
Grandson/ Granddaughter	What else can you think of?

ROLES (CONTINUED)

I will talk about what other roles/tasks I have, my parents have, and my brother/sister has. Write them here:

. . . .

. . . .

. . . .

. . . .

. . . .

. . . .

. . . .

. . . .

. . . .

. . . .

Sometimes you have to be a role that you don't like. Talk to each other about why you have those roles and whether you like them or not. You can cross out the ones you don't like and circle the ones you do like.

FAMILY MEMBERS

People are a part of life. There are people at home and at school. There are children, teenagers, adults, and elderly people. There are people in stores, in cars, and on the street. Sometimes they are alone, and sometimes they are in groups.

Most children live with their families. Some children live with one parent. Some children live with two parents. Some children have stepparents. My parents' and siblings' names are:

. . . .

. . . .

. . . .

. . . .

Sometimes you have grandparents, aunts, uncles, cousins, or friends that you see often or help your family with different things. List those people here:

. . . .

. . . .

. . . .

. . . .

. . . .

FAMILY MEMBERS (CONTINUED)

Sometimes family members help with different roles in my family. I will talk about the family members who help and what roles they help with. I will circle the roles that I like them helping with and cross out the ones that I don't like them helping with. I can write them here:

. . . .

. . . .

. . . .

. . . .

. . . .

We will talk about what roles I wish my family would help with or stop helping with. I can write those below:

. . . .

. . . .

. . . .

. . . .

. . . .

. . . .

NEW OR DIFFERENT PEOPLE

Sometimes, new or different people come into the classroom. Some children are happy to meet new people and make new friends. They think it is fun. Other children might become anxious, worried, scared, or angry when there are changes with people at school. At first, siblings might not like these kinds of changes.

It may take more time for a sibling to get used to new people or make new friends because they worry about how that person might treat their brother/sister with autism.

I will write how I teach new people about autism below. If I am not sure how, I can ask my parents to help.

. . . .

. . . .

. . . .

. . . .

. . . .

. . . .

. . . .

. . . .

Chapter Six

Understanding

WORKBOOK

Eye Contact

Eye contact means looking directly at someone's eyes. Many children listen and understand better when they look directly into the eyes of the person who is talking. Most children make eye contact when they are paying attention to someone talking to them. That is why people think that if you make eye contact, you will understand them better. When you don't make eye contact, they think you are not paying attention. This is true for many children, but it may not be true for many children with autism.

Many people with autism:

- Find it difficult to make eye contact AND listen.

- Find it difficult to understand what a person is saying when they have to look at their eyes.

- Think it is easier to understand someone if they look somewhere else.

**I will circle what is true for me and highlight
was is true for my brother/sister:**

I can make eye contact or I can listen, but it is difficult to do
both at the same time.

It is difficult to understand what the person is saying when I
have to look at their eyes.

It is easier for me to understand what people are saying when I
look somewhere else.

I do not like eye contact because it is uncomfortable.

Sometimes I like to make eye contact and listen at the
same time.

WORDS: LITERAL MEANINGS AND FIGURES OF SPEECH

Some words and phrases have two meanings. The first meaning is literal. Literal is when the word means exactly what it says.

But sometimes, people use figures of speech. These phrases actually mean something different than what is literally said.

For example:

'Hit the road' doesn't mean to literally hit the road. When people say 'hit the road,' it means it is time to go somewhere else.

'Off the wall' doesn't really mean that something is off of the wall. When people say 'off the wall,' it means something is unusual or odd.

'Straighten up' doesn't really mean that someone needs to stand straight up. When people say 'straighten up,' it means they want you to have good behavior and follow the rules.

Below I will write figures of speech I use often and then draw or write what it might mean literally for my brother/sister.

Figures of Speech

What it means for my Brother/ Sister

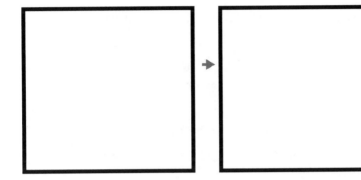

Body Language and Facial Expressions

People communicate by talking and writing. People also communicate by moving their faces and their bodies. When they communicate by moving their bodies, it is called body language. When they communicate by moving their faces, it is called using facial expressions.

The meaning of body language and facial expressions is not always exact, but most non-autistic children understand them automatically. I can see that people move their bodies and faces, but I may not always know what it means. Understanding body language and facial expressions may not come naturally for children with autism.

Look through magazines for pictures of people's faces with different expressions and paste them below.

Happy Face	Sad Face
Worried Face	Excited Face

UNIQUE

Everyone has something unique about them. Unique means something that makes a person different than everyone else. Some people have more differences than others. Differences help make us unique.

Below I will share what makes me unique in this color:

. . . .

. . . .

. . . .

I will share what makes my brother unique in this color:

. . . .

. . . .

. . . .

If we both have the same thing that makes us unique from most people I will put it in this color:

. . . .

. . . .

. . . .

. . . .

Date . . . .

HELPING OTHERS UNDERSTAND

An advocate is someone who stands up for others. As a sibling, I have always been an advocate for my brother/sister with autism. This includes talking to friends about why my brother/sister might act a certain way or explaining to a new babysitter how things happen.

I am an advocate for my family when I:

. . . .

. . . .

. . . .

Another way I can be an advocate is by using my talents. If I am able to draw, I can create pictures that share information about what autism is to me. If I am great at writing, I can write about my experiences. If I enjoy cooking, I can donate my time to an autism organization for a fundraiser.

WRITE IT. DRAW IT. PASTE IT. Below I will share my favorite talent and how I can use it to be an advocate:

Awareness Campaigns

I can also raise awareness by being a part of campaigns. A campaign is when you have multiple people come together to raise awareness about a certain topic. I can create my own or be a part of another one.

Campaign Name:

I want to raise awareness for autism and/or being a sibling because:

. . . .

. . . .

I will create . . . .

to raise awareness and share them at . . . .

I will ask these people to help me:

. . . .

. . . .

Our goal will be:

. . . .

. . . .

Chapter Seven

THOUGHTS

WORKBOOK

WHAT ARE THOUGHTS?

Thoughts are what I see or hear or feel in my mind:

- When I remember something that has happened, when I see a picture in my mind.

- When I remember how something felt, when I think words quietly to myself.

Everyone has thoughts. Thoughts are words or pictures or feelings in other people's minds, too.

Here I am. I will write some thoughts I have had today, in the thinking bubble.

WHO HAS THOUGHTS?

I have thoughts. My parent has thoughts. Brothers and sisters have thoughts. Grandparents have thoughts. My teacher has thoughts. Children have thoughts. Teenagers have thoughts. Adults have thoughts.

Everyone has thoughts.

WRITE IT. DRAW IT. PASTE IT. Here are some thoughts that I think my family might have:

Date . . . .

HOPES ARE THOUGHTS

Hopes are thoughts about what I want to happen. It may feel good to think about my hopes. Sometimes what I hope for may happen soon, and sometimes it happens much later. Sometimes what I hope for never happens at all. Sometimes, there might be things that I can do to help make my hopes happen, someday.

WRITE IT. DRAW IT. PASTE IT. Below are my hopes:

No one knows my hopes unless I tell them or show them what my hopes are. I can tell my hopes to these important people in my life:

1. . . . .

2. . . . .

3. . . . .

4. . . . .

5. . . . .

FEARS ARE THOUGHTS

Fears are thoughts that make me feel afraid or worried. Everyone has fears, sometimes.

Sometimes I feel afraid when I don't know what is going to happen. Sometimes I feel afraid when my brother/sister is upset.

When I have fears or when I am afraid, I can tell my fears to someone who cares about me. My parent and my teacher care about me. But they don't know my fear unless I tell them or unless I write it down and show them what I have written. Here are the names of some of the important people whom I can talk to or write to when I am afraid:

1. . . . .

2. . . . .

3. . . . .

4. . . . .

5. . . . .

These people will not make fun of me for being afraid. They know that everyone feels fear sometimes. They will listen to me.

WRITE IT. DRAW IT. PASTE IT. Below are my fears:

SIBLING'S THOUGHTS

Being a sibling of someone with autism, I sometimes have different thoughts than my peers.

I worry about my brother/sister while they are at school, with friends, traveling, and many more things.

WRITE IT. DRAW IT. PASTE IT. Below are thoughts that I have. I will circle the ones that are unique to me because I have a brother/ sister with autism.

Chapter Eight

COMMUNICATION

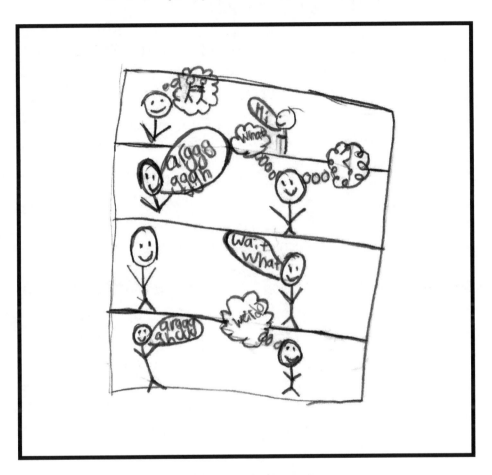

WORKBOOK

THE PROCESS OF COMMUNICATION

The process of communication is like a circle:

- Putting my thoughts into words.

- Getting someone's attention and telling them the words.

- Listening to what that person is saying back to me.

- Thinking about what that person said.

- Putting my next thoughts (about what the person said) into words.

- Telling them the words… And continuing on…

Sometimes my brother/sister with autism has a difficult time communicating or I have a difficult time communicating with them. I know my brother/sister communicates better when:

. . . .

. . . .

I know my brother/sister has a hard time communicating when:

. . . .

. . . .

When I want to talk to my brother/sister about something important, I can try to use their favorite way of communication.

PUTTING MY THOUGHTS INTO WORDS

When I want to talk to my brother/sister about something important, I can try different ways to communicate.

I can try to:

- Draw a comic strip if I am trying to explain a story to my brother/sister.

- Take a picture of something I want him/her to see.

- Create a sheet with multiple different images. When I want him to tell me something or understand something, I can use the images to help him understand.

Here are some ways I can try to communicate:

. . . .

. . . .

. . . .

. . . .

As a family, we will try the methods that we think will work the best. I will write the one we like the most here:

. . . .

. . . .

PUTTING MY THOUGHTS INTO WORDS (CONTINUED)

Sometimes I have something that I want or need to say to my parents but I might not be able to tell them right away. I might not be able to tell them right away because they have to help my brother/sister with autism, or I would rather write it down instead of talk to them about it, or something else.

One way that I can get out my feelings right away is by sharing a journal that is just for me and my parents.

Below I will circle the rules for our journal:

- We can only read what the other person wrote when the journal is put in our special place.

- We won't be mad when responding in the journal. If we are mad, we will wait to respond until we are no longer mad.

- We won't try to talk to each other about what is written in the journal unless there is a star written at the end of the entry. The star means that you can respond by writing or by talking.

- We can write anything in the journal, even if it is simply to tell each other our love for them.

- We will make sure to check the journal every day.

Here are some other rules for our journal:

. . . .

. . . .

. . . .

. . . .

. . . .

. . . .

. . . .

. . . .

. . . .

. . . .

. . . .

. . . .

. . . .

. . . .

SENTENCE STARTERS

These sentence starters might be useful to me. I can turn to this page when I want to say something but I'm not sure how to begin. My parent, teacher, or therapist can make me a copy of this page. I can use extra paper, so there will be more room to write my thoughts in words. Or, I may type on a keyboard. My parent, teacher, or therapist may write other sentence starters for me, too.

I want to . . . .

Please help me with . . . .

The teacher said that . . . .

At school, I . . . .

What does '. . . . .' mean?

Someone said that . . . .

I am thinking about . . . .

Is it true that . . . . ?

I hope that. . . . .

I am really happy that . . . .

I don't understand about . . . .

There is something I'd like to do. It is. . . . .

Thank you for . . . .

COMMUNICATING FEELINGS

Talking about your feelings can be difficult, especially when you don't want to add any stress. In Chapter 11, we will talk more about feeling upset.

When I want to tell someone how I feel about something, I can:

- Ask them to sit down.

- Make sure they are listening.

- Wait until I know I will be able to listen to them, also.

Sometimes communicating feelings can be scary. I will make sure that I prepare myself by doing one of my favorite talents.

WRITE IT. DRAW IT. PASTE IT. Below I will put how I feel about trying to communicate feelings to people:

WRITING LETTERS

There are people at school or in my family who upset me because of how they treat me, my brother/sister with autism, or my parents. There are also people who make me really happy because of how they treat us. Writing letters to let those people know how I feel can make it easier for everyone to understand our emotions better. It can also help us with our communication.

Below I will write a letter to someone who I want to tell about autism:

. . . .

. . . .

. . . .

. . . .

. . . .

. . . .

. . . .

. . . .

. . . .

. . . .

COMMUNICATING WITH ART

Some people like to express themselves creatively. They like to communicate with art.

If I try to communicate my ideas and thoughts with art, I have to remember that people who see or hear my art will think their own thoughts. When they hear or read or see my art, their ideas might be different from what I want to communicate. They might not understand exactly what I am trying to express.

If I want my parent, teacher, or friends to know something important, I can do it through art, but then I also need to do one of these things:

- Put it in words and tell the person.

- Write it down in words and give it to the person.

- Type it and show it to the person.

- Send the words by mail or e-mail to the person.

I can still enjoy doing my art, but I should also try to communicate in one of those four ways.

Below I will draw something that I want my family to know about my day and a sentence or two about the picture:

Chapter Nine

School

WORKBOOK

Date . . . .

School Boundaries

Sometimes I get anxious about going to school because I worry about my brother/sister with autism. Being taken out of class or having to worry about my brother/sister with autism can make it difficult for me to concentrate.

Below I will circle the things that are true for me. I worry that:

- Someone will be mean to my brother/sister.

- An adult won't understand my brother/sister so they'll get in trouble.

- Someone will be mean to me because of my brother/ sister.

- I will be taken out of my class to help my brother/sister.

Here are some other things that I worry about:

. . . .

. . . .

. . . .

. . . .

. . . .

. . . .

. . . .

Below I will circle what is true for me. I would like to know that when I go to school I:

- Will not be taken out of class.

- Am able to have a safe place to go if anyone is mean or I need to talk.

- Will not be talked to by adults about what my brother/ sister is doing.

I would also like:

. . . .

. . . .

. . . .

. . . .

. . . .

. . . .

. . . .

. . . .

. . . .

. . . .

Safe Place

Sometimes when I'm at school, I might need someone to talk to about what is happening. Below, I will write some people or places where I feel safe at school. We can talk to my school about how I can make sure I am able to talk to that safe person or go to that safe place when I am feeling anxious.

. . . .

. . . .

. . . .

. . . .

. . . .

. . . .

. . . .

. . . .

. . . .

. . . .

. . . .

LETTER TO MY BROTHER/SISTER'S TEACHER

Being a sibling means that I have a unique view of what my brother/sister with autism is like. Sometimes what I know about my brother/sister can help other people better understand him/her. Below I will write a letter to his/her teacher that I can keep or give to his/her teacher to help them better understand my brother/sister:

Dear . . . . ,

. . . .

. . . .

. . . .

. . . .

. . . .

. . . .

. . . .

. . . .

. . . .

. . . .

Date . . . .

Letter to My Teacher

I have unique needs being a sibling to someone with autism.
Not everyone understands what makes my life different. Below
I will write a letter to my teacher that I can keep or give to
him/her to help them better understand me:

Dear . . . . ,

. . . .

. . . .

. . . .

. . . .

. . . .

. . . .

. . . .

. . . .

. . . .

. . . .

. . . .

Awareness at School

I want people to better understand what autism is.

Below I will write who I want to learn more about autism:

. . . .

. . . .

I want people to know this about autism:

. . . .

. . . .

. . . .

I want them to learn about autism by:

. . . .

. . . .

I can help them learn about autism by:

. . . .

. . . .

. . . .

. . . .

Chapter Ten

FRIENDS

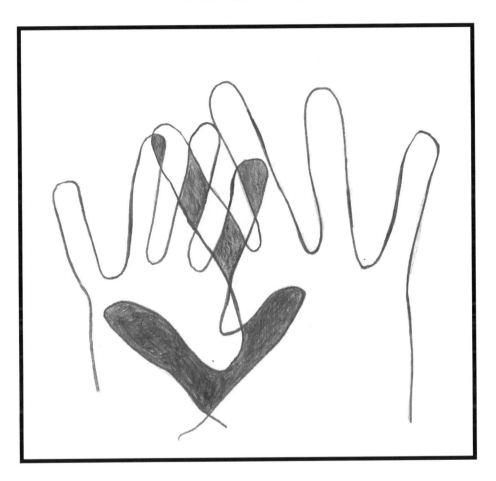

WORKBOOK

WHAT IS A FRIEND?

A friend is a person who is not in my family but who is important to me, in a good way.

A friend is important because both of us like each other. Friends like to spend time together sometimes. We like to do many of the same things.

These are things I'd like to do with a friend:

1. . . . .

2. . . . .

3. . . . .

4. . . . .

5. . . . .

Other children might not understand some of the things my brother/sister does or some of the things they say.

One part of being a friend is trying to understand each other.

A friend might understand my brother/sister better if he or she knows they have autism. I can help her or him understand autism.

When I make a friend, I tell them this about my brother/sister:

A friend usually does not make fun of me or my family.
A true friend is nice to me and my family. I try to be nice to
my friends, too.

A Friend Coming to My House

Below I will circle what is true for me:

- I invite friends to my house all the time.

- I only invite certain friends to my house.

- I don't invite friends to my house because I am worried about how they will treat my brother/sister.

- I don't invite friends to my house because I am worried about how my brother/sister will act.

If I want to have a friend come to my house, I can get ready by following this checklist:

☑ My parent and I can make a list of concerns or expectations.

☑ Discuss how to handle each concern or expectation.

☑ Talk to my friend about my brother/sister with autism.

WRITE IT. DRAW IT. PASTE IT. Below is an image that represents what a perfect day with my friend would look like:

Having a Mentor

A mentor is a special kind of friend. A mentor is an adult who likes me and likes the same things I like. Spending time with a mentor may be fun. A mentor can be a good friend, especially as a child grows into an adult.

- A mentor can help me learn more about myself and help me learn more about the world.

- A mentor can try to answer questions and help me find the answers.

- A mentor can encourage me with my hopes and dreams and can help me find good ways to use my talents, skills, and special interests.

- A mentor may also be a sibling of someone with autism, or maybe not.

I might have a mentor someday. A mentor is usually not my parent, but my parent can help me find a mentor. A mentor might be a teacher, a friend of my parent, an aunt, an uncle, or someone else.

I will mark what is true for me:

☐ I would like to have a mentor.

☐ I have a mentor whose name is

☐ Other:

WRITE IT. DRAW IT. PASTE IT. Below are things that I hope my mentor enjoys or helps me learn more about:

Chapter Eleven

FEELING UPSET

WORKBOOK

FEELING EMOTIONS

People feel emotions inside of them. My emotions are feelings I have inside of me.

Examples of words to describe emotions are happy, joyful, sad, angry, frustrated, scared, worried, and

. . . .

WRITE IT. DRAW IT. PASTE IT. Below are all the feelings that I have had today:

Date . . . .

FEELING ANXIOUS

Everyone feels anxious sometimes. Anxious means that a child or adult feels worried, uneasy, and restless. The person's hands might tremble, or he may cry, or he might get a stomachache or a headache. Sometimes he might want to run or hide. Sometimes feeling anxious turns into anger, and a person might want to yell or lash out. Or, a person might get very quiet when feeling anxious.

I will circle what is true for me.

I feel anxious when:

- My brother/sister with autism is going to a new place.

- We go to dinner as a family.

- When we go to an appointment.

- My brother/sister with autism is upset.

- When I don't know what is going on.

WRITE IT. DRAW IT. PASTE IT. Below I will create an image that represents how I feel when I am anxious:

BEING OPPOSITIONAL

Being oppositional means that someone refuses to do what their parent or teacher or someone else wants them to do. It is called oppositional because the person does or says the opposite of what someone wants them to do.

Children and teenagers who are like this often are described as being oppositional.

Some children become oppositional when they are anxious or upset. Sometimes it becomes a habit.

I will circle what is true for me.

I can be oppositional when:

- I feel like I'm not getting enough attention.

- I am tired.

- I am anxious or upset about something that is going on.

WRITE IT. DRAW IT. PASTE IT. Below I will create an image that represents how other people feel when I'm being oppositional:

HURTING MYSELF

Once in a while, some siblings may try to hurt themselves. Parents and teachers and other people feel very worried when children hurt themselves. This is called self-injurious behavior, or SIB.

IF I NEVER TRY TO HURT MYSELF, THEN I DO NOT HAVE TO READ MORE ON THIS PAGE. I CAN TURN TO THE NEXT PAGE.

When I am thinking about hurting myself, I need to take the following steps:

- Find a safe person. (Parent, teacher, family member, etc.)

- Tell them I want to hurt myself.

- Tell them why I want to.

- Ask them to help me find a better way to handle the situation.

WRITE IT. DRAW IT. PASTE IT. Below my parents and I will put down different ways that I can handle those situations. We can try different things like yoga, reading, drawing, or any other kind of activity that might relieve my stress.

HURTING OTHER PEOPLE

Once in a while, children may hit, kick, or scratch other people. They may throw things. This is called aggression or being aggressive, and it hurts other people or other things. Parents and teachers are very worried when children are aggressive.

Sometimes our brother/sister with autism can be aggressive. Usually, most people with autism do not want to hurt anyone on purpose. They probably didn't plan to hurt someone. But, sometimes, a child with autism may be very upset or angry and may hurt someone who is nearby.

WRITE IT. DRAW IT. PASTE IT. Below I will show new ways to handle my feelings when I feel like being aggressive or my brother/sister is being aggressive:

EMOTION-METER FOR MY PARENT

To the parent or teacher or other significant adult:

This is for you to fill out about yourself, to communicate to your child more accurately what you are feeling about an incident or situation. Fill in the information to describe what you are feeling. Then indicate the level or degree that most accurately describes the intensity of your emotion in this particular situation. Color it in like a thermometer. Show it to your child to help him accurately get the right message, to read how and what you are feeling about the situation.

Parent's Name: . . . .

The situation: . . . .

. . . .

The emotion: . . . .

The emotion-meter reading:

The biggest, most intense feeling — 3

In the middle—some feeling, but not too much — 2

Just a tiny bit of feeling — 1

Date . . . .

EMOTION-METER FOR ME

I will mark what is true for me.

1. Describe the situation and the emotion, in the boxes below:

> The situation (with whom, about what, where, and when)

> The emotion (circle the word or write on the lines)
>
> Happy   Sad   Worried   Angry   Scared   Frustrated
>
> Or . . . . and . . . .

2. The emotion-meter reading:

The biggest, most intense feeling ─ 3

In the middle—some feeling, but not too much ─ 2

Just a tiny bit of feeling ─ 1

3. What I can do when I am feeling…:

. . . .

. . . .

COUNSELING

Counseling is when a person goes to an office to talk or type computer conversations with a counselor or therapist. Sometimes counseling can help a person learn how to feel less anxious and how to feel better.

Sometimes going to see a counselor or therapist can make someone anxious.

WRITE IT. DRAW IT. PASTE IT. To help not be anxious when you go to the counselor or therapist for the first time, I will create something for them to better understand myself:

FEELING BETTER

I can create a toolbox that I can use to feel better when I am anxious or upset.

This toolbox can include:

- A journal to write or draw in.

- Markers or pens.

- Something I like to hold.

- Something I like to smell.

- Something I like to taste.

- Something I like to look at.

- Something I like to listen to.

- A book to read.

- A coloring book.

- A note from someone I love.

- What else???

I will circle the different techniques that I would like to try:

- Yoga.

- Meditating.

- Exercising.

- Listening/Playing Music.

- Coloring.

WRITE IT. DRAW IT. PASTE IT. Below I will put some other ideas I have to feel better:

Chapter Twelve

HAPPINESS

A FEELING OF WELL-BEING

WORKBOOK

WHAT IS HAPPINESS?

Happiness is not something that can be physically touched...
it is invisible. It is a feeling inside of a person. Some people
describe it as a soft or light feeling. It could be described as a
calm, peaceful, and satisfied feeling. It could be a feeling that is
joyful or cheerful.

Happiness is a feeling of well-being. Most people like
feeling happiness. When they feel sadness or another
uncomfortable feeling, they usually want to know how to
feel better and happier.

WRITE IT. DRAW IT. PASTE IT. Below I will create a representation of
happiness to me:

Exercise the Heart Muscle

Cardiovascular exercise keeps my body strong and helps me stay healthy. It is good to exercise once (or twice) each day, for about 20–30 minutes or more, with a good, fast heartbeat. This kind of exercise is called cardiovascular (or cardio, for short) and may help me stay calmer throughout the day. Exercise is one of the things that helps create well-being or happiness.

I will mark the kind of cardio exercises I would like to do:

☐ Walking fast or running or jogging.

☐ Running up a hill and rolling down.

☐ Jumping on a trampoline.

☐ Swimming.

☐ Dancing to music.

☐ Riding a bicycle or a stationary bike.

☐ Jumping rope or a pogo stick.

☐ Rollerskating.

☐ Horseback riding.

☐ Walking up a snowy hill and sledding down.

☐ Snowshoeing or cross-country skiing.

☐ Other: . . . .

I will highlight the activities that I want to do by myself and circle the ones I want to do with my entire family.

STRETCHING

Stretching keeps my body flexible and helps me stay healthy. Stretching is when I slowly and carefully move a part of my body and hold it for a count of 12 seconds or more. It feels good for my muscles, and it may help me feel calmer.

My parent, teacher, or mentor can help me find pictures of stretches I can do at school and at home. I should take a stretch break a few times each day. Stretching should feel good and not hurt. (If it hurts, I should stop and tell my parent, teacher, or therapist.) Stretching is one of the things that helps generate a feeling of calmness and well-being.

Check with a physical therapist or other health professional to learn about these:

- ☐ Using rubber resistance bands.
- ☐ Doing specific stretches while sitting at a desk or on a chair.
- ☐ Doing specific stretches while standing.
- ☐ Doing specific stretches while lying on the floor.
- ☐ Stretching upper-body muscles and lower-body muscles.
- ☐ Taking stretch breaks during school.
- ☐ Taking stretch breaks at home.
- ☐ Doing yoga postures.
- ☐ Other: . . . .

I will highlight the activities that I want to do by myself and circle the ones I want to do with my entire family.

RELAXATION

Relaxation is the word to describe when my body and my mind are calm. Most people have to learn how to relax.

Relaxation is one of the most valuable ways to help a person feel happiness or a sense of well-being.

I can mark some things to try:

- ☐ Go to my safe place.
- ☐ Listen to my favorite calming music.
- ☐ Practice slow, deep breathing.
- ☐ Practice a tensing-and-relaxing muscle routine.
- ☐ Listen to music and guided visualizations.
- ☐ Watch a video that shows me a relaxation routine.
- ☐ Watch a video with my favorite things.
- ☐ Sit quietly and do nothing at all.
- ☐ Relax while stretching.
- ☐ Get (or give) a massage.
- ☐ Swing (in the basement, the yard, or a park).
- ☐ Other: . . . .

I will highlight the activities that I want to do by myself and circle the ones I want to do with my entire family.

SLEEP

Getting enough sleep helps me feel rested. Sleep gives me more energy when I am awake. Getting enough sleep helps me feel better and get through the day.

Having a regular sleep pattern is one of the things that helps me to have a feeling of well-being or happiness.

For better sleep, we can try these ideas:

- ☐ Follow an evening routine.
- ☐ Take a warm bath in the evening.
- ☐ Wake up at the same time each day.
- ☐ Use heavy curtains to keep out light/noise.
- ☐ Open the curtains at sunrise to let the light come in.
- ☐ Use a white-noise machine.
- ☐ Use a weighted blanket.
- ☐ Sleep in a sleeping bag in a little tent.
- ☐ Bedtime routine includes calming music.
- ☐ Finish watching TV or using electronic devices an hour before bedtime.
- ☐ Avoid food with caffeine, sugar, and additives 2 hours before bed.
- ☐ Get enough exercise during the day.
- ☐ Other: . . . .

BEING KIND

Being kind helps people feel happy. The person who does a kind thing feels happier. The person who receives a kind thing feels happier, too. Here are some examples of being kind:

- Saying good morning to someone.

- Spending time petting or playing with an animal friend.

- Smiling.

- Holding the door open for someone.

- Sending someone a friendly card or note.

- Sending a "get well" card to a sick person.

- Helping someone if they ask for help.

- Saying "Can I help you?" if a person is carrying things.

- Using good manners: Saying "please" and "thank you."

- Thanking someone for something they did for me.

- Other examples from my life: . . . .

. . . .

. . . .

. . . .

WRITE IT. DRAW IT. PASTE IT. Below I will create an image that represents how I feel when I'm kind to someone or someone is kind to me:

Fitting in or Being My Unique Self

No one is exactly the same. Every person is different from one another. Everyone is unique.

Every person has unique ways of being themselves.

But many people, especially children about the age of 10 years all the way through the teenage years, until the ages of 20 or even older, try to look and act and talk the same as each other. They think it is better to be the same as each other, even if it is not their natural way of being. This is called 'fitting in.' Many children try to 'fit in' instead of feeling comfortable being their unique selves.

There are some children who do not care if they 'fit in.' Sometimes children try to 'fit in,' but they may not know what to do or how to 'fit in.'

Trying to 'fit in' is not very fun.
It is better to be yourself... and to grow into being your best self!

I am unique.

It is perfectly OK to be me, just the way I am.

Date . . . .

WRITE IT. DRAW IT. PASTE IT. Below are all the great things that make me unique: